Curries From The North

By

Aroona Reejhsinghani

V&S PUBLISHERS

Published by:

V&S PUBLISHERS

F-2/16, Ansari Road, Daryaganj, New Delhi-110002
☎ 011-23240026, 011-23240027 • *Fax* 011-23240028
Email info@vspublishers.com • *Website* www.vspublishers.com

Regional Office Hyderabad
5-1-707/1, Brij Bhawan (Beside Central Bank of India Lane)
Bank Street, Koti, Hyderabad - 500 095
☎ 040-24737290
E-mail vspublishershyd@gmail.com

Branch Office Mumbai
Jaywant Industrial Estate, 2nd Floor–222, Tardeo Road
Opposite Sobo Central Mall, Mumbai – 400 034
☎ 022-23510736
E-mail: vspublishersmum@gmail.com

Follow us on: 🇹 🇫

All books available at **www.vspublishers.com**

CONTENTS

Introduction

India is famous for its curries. In fact, it is the home of an endless variety of curries, each better than the other. Indians relish hundreds of curries made with vegetables, meat, fish, prawn and eggs. Every Zone in India has its own special way of preparing curries, therefore, each curry has a unique flavour. In Punjabi curries, coconut is rarely used. Curries are always served with plain fluffy boiled rice and papads which are either fried or roasted.

In India, majority of the people are vegetarian, hence there is a greater variety of delicious vegetarian curries prepared with dals and a variety of vegetables, curds and buttermilk. But this does not mean that there is very little to choose in case of non-vegetarian curries. Indian meat curries, in fact, take many forms. Like kofta curries, ground meat is shaped into balls and cooked in a deliciously rich sauce or curry. Then, there are korma curries — spicy and delicious, keema curries — which is ground meat cooked with peas and decorated with hard-boiled eggs.

In this book, I have chosen for you a wide variety of flavours — some simple, some exotic, some extraordinarily delicious. This book contains recipes for some special curries made and enjoyed in North Zone of India. The aim is to make people relish curries of a particular region even if they don't belong to that region. Even the foreigners can try these recipes to relish a unique taste. Here for you is a distinctive selection of curries which are as distinctive as different wines in different bottles.

Aroona Reejhsinghani
502 B, Lila Apts.
opp. Gul Mohar Gardens,
Yari Road, Versova
Bombay-61
Ph – 6360224

1

Punjabi Curries

Punjabis are acclaimed as gourmets the world over. Their fondness for rich food has led to the development of an abundant variety of spicy and colourful curries. In Punjabi curries, vegetables do play an important role, therefore many of their vegetarian curries are quite unique. Some curries are particular to Punjab, like pakoda curry which is prepared by cooking round fluffy balls of gramflour in a rich yellow curd curry. Non-vegetarian Punjabi curries mostly comprising fish, chicken and mutton have distinct Mughlai influence on them in appearance and taste. They will satisfy any gourmet.

VEGETARIAN CURRIES

BESAN KOFTA CURRY

Ingredients (Serves 4)

- 1 large onion
- 4 flakes of garlic
- 2 big tomatoes, pureed
- 1 tsp. garam masala
- 1/4 tsp. turmeric powder
- 1 tblsp. dhania-jeera powder
- Salt and chilli powder to taste

For Koftas

- 250 grams besan or gram flour
- 1/2 tsp. cumin seeds
- 1½ tblsps. melted ghee
- 1 tsp. crushed pomegranate seeds
- 100 grams grated onions
- Alubhukharas or dry plums, seeded

Preparation

Mix together all the kofta ingredients except plums, without adding water. Turn the ingredients paste into balls around the whole plums. Deep fry the balls to a golden colour. Grind onion and garlic to a paste. Heat 2 tbslps. ghee and fry the ground paste to a golden colour. Add to the paste all the spices and tomatoes and cook till the ghee separates. Then add 2 cups of water, bring slowly to a boil and keep boiling gently for 5 minutes. Then add koftas and boil for 5 more minutes. Serve hot decorated with coriander leaves.

DAHI KOFTA CURRY

Ingredients (Serves 6)

- 2 large tomatoes, pureed
- 1 large onion
- 8 flakes of garlic
- 1/4 coconut
- 1 tblsp. dhania-jeera powder
- 1/4 tsp. turmeric powder
- Handful of coriander leaves
- Salt and chilli powder to taste

For Koftas

- 250 grams curd
- 50 grams gramflour or besan
- 25 grams mixed finely sliced nuts like almonds, raisins, cashewnuts, walnuts, pistachios
- 1 tsp. grated ginger
- 1/4 tsp. garam masala
- Handful of chopped coriander leaves
- Salt , lime juice and chilli powder to taste

Preparation

Grind nuts, ginger and coriander leaves to a paste. Mix with garam masala, salt and lime juice and set aside. Put curd in a clean piece of cloth and tie loosely. Hang the bag for a couple of hours to make all the liquid drip through. Mix salt, curd and gramflour, and knead to a smooth mixture. Form the mixture into small balls around the ground paste made earlier. Deep fry the balls to golden colour. Grind onions, garlic and coconut to a paste. Heat 4 tblsps. ghee and fry the paste to a golden colour. Add to the fried paste, spices and tomatoes and cook till ghee separates. Then add 2 cups of water, bring the mixture to a boil, and keep boiling for 5 minutes. Now put in koftas, reduce heat to simmering and boil for 5 more minutes. Decorate with chopped coriander leaves.

BHIEN CURRY

Ingredients (Serves 4)

- 250 grams bhien or lotus stems
- 250 grams peas, boiled
- 100 grams tomatoes, pureed
- 4 flakes of garlic, 1 large onion
- 1 tblsp. dhania-jeera powder
- 4 green slit chillies
- Handful of coriander leaves
- A few curry leaves
- 1/4 tsp turmeric powder
- 1/4 tsp. garam masala
- Salt and chilli powder to taste

Preparation

Clean, wash, slice and boil bhien. Grind onion and garlic to a paste. Heat 3 tblsps. ghee and fry the paste to a golden colour. Add tomatoes, spices, curry leaves and chillies to the fried paste and cook till the ghee separates. Then add vegetables, mix well and then pour in the coconut milk. Simmer over a gentle fire till the curry turns a little thick. Decorate with chopped coriander leaves.

BHIEN KOFTA CURRY

Ingredients (Serves 5)

For Koftas

- 250 grams bhien, cleaned, sliced and boiled
- 1 small onion minced
- Handful of coriander leaves
- 2 green chillies, minced
- 3 tblsps. gramflour or besan
- A few mint leaves
- 1/2 tsp. ground cumin seeds
- Salt and chilli powder to taste

For Curry

- 2 big onions
- 8 flakes of garlic
- 4 big tomatoes
- 3 tblsps. beaten cream
- 1/4 tsp. turmeric powder
- 1 tblsp dhania-jeera powder
- Handful of coriander leaves
- Salt and chilli powder to taste

Preparation

Grind bhien to a smooth paste. Mix in all the kofta ingredients and form into small balls. Deep fry to a golden colour. Grind onion and garlic to a paste. Heat 3 tblsps. ghee and fry the paste to a golden colour. Add to the golden paste, spices and tomatoes and cook till the ghee oozes out. Then add 2 cups of water. Bring the mixture to a boil, reduce heat and put in the koftas. Boil over a slow fire for 5 minutes. Mix in cream and decorate with coriander leaves. Serve hot.

PUMPKIN KOFTA CURRY

Ingredients (Serves 6)

For Curry

- 2 cups coconut milk
- 1 cup nicely beaten curd
- 100 grams grated tomatoes
- 1 tsp. each of ginger and garlic paste
- 1 big onion, grated
- 1/2 tsp. garam masala
- 1 tblsp. dhania-jeera powder
- 1/4 tsp. turmeric powder
- Handful of coriander leaves
- Salt and chilli powder to taste

For Koftas

- 1/2 kilo peeled and grated pumpkin or doodhi
- 3 tblsps. wheat flour
- 1 small onion, minced
- 1/2 tsp. minced ginger
- 2 green chillies, minced
- Handful of sliced coriander leaves
- Salt and chilli powder to taste

Preparation

Squeeze out water from pumpkin. Mix it in all the kofta ingredients and form into balls. Deep fry the balls to a golden colour. Heat 3 tblsps. ghee and fry ginger, garlic and onions to a golden colour. Add to it tomatoes and spices and fry till the ghee oozes out. Mix in curd and coconut milk, heat gently, add koftas and simmer gently for a few minutes. Decorate with coriander leaves.

PAKODA CURRY

Ingredients (Serves 6)

For Curry

- 1/2 kilo sour curd
- 1/4 tsp. each of fenugreek, mustard and cumin seeds
- Dash of asafoetida
- 6 green slit chillies
- 1/2 tsp. turmeric powder
- A couple of curry leaves
- 1 tblsp. minced ginger
- 1 medium onion, minced
- 2 tblsps. gramflour or besan
- 1 large tomato, sliced
- Salt to taste

For Pakodas

- 100 grams gramflour or besan
- 1 tblsp crushed pomegranate seeds
- A few sliced mint leaves
- 2 green chillies minced
- 1 tsp. ginger minced
- 1 small potato, 1 small cauliflower, 1 small carrot
- 2 tblsps. boiled peas
- Salt to taste
- A pinch of soda bicarbonate

Preparation

Chop the vegetables very finely. Mix all the pakoda ingredients together along with enough water to form thick batter. Drop teaspoonfuls of batter in smoking ghee and fry to a golden colour. Heat 3 tblsp. ghee and fry mustard, fenugreek, cumin seeds and hing. Add onion, ginger, curry leaves and fry till soft. Add tomatoes, spices and salt. Fry till the ghee oozes out, then put in curd beaten with 4 cups water and mixed with gramflour. Add salt, turmeric and chillies. Bring slowly to a boil, reduce heat and simmer gently for 5 minutes Now add pakodas. Simmer till curry turns a little thick. Decorate with coriander leaves, and sprinkle garam masala on top.

ZAMIKAND KOFTA CURRY

Ingredients (Serves 5)

For Koftas

- 250 grams Zamikand or yam
- 100 grams paneer
- 2 tblsps. cornflour
- 1 tblsp. mango powder
- Handful of coriander leaves
- 2 green chillies, minced
- 1/2 tsp. grated ginger
- Salt to taste

For Curry

- 3 big tomatoes, grated
- 2 tblsps. powdered cashew nuts
- 1 onion, grated
- 1 tsp. each of grated ginger and garlic.
- Handful of chopped coriander leaves
- 2 tblsps. cream
- 1/2 tsp. garam masala
- 1/4 tsp. turmeric powder
- 1 tblsp. dhania-jeera powder
- Salt and chilli powder to taste

Preparation

Boil zamikand, mash it to a paste and mix with cornflour and salt. Mix the remaining kofta ingredients with paneer. Divide zamikand into small portions and form into koftas or balls around the paneer mixture. Deep fry the balls to a golden colour. Heat 3 tblsps. oil and fry onions, ginger and garlic till soft. Add to the fried contents tomatoes, salt, spices and cashewnuts. Keep frying till the oil comes out. Then add 2 cups water. Cook for two minutes, then mix in the cream and pour the mixture over the koftas. Sprinkle garam masala on top and decorate with coriander leaves.

MUSHROOM CURRY

Ingredients (Serves 4)

- 250 grams mushrooms, cut into four pieces each
- 50 grams powdered cashewnuts
- 5-6 almonds, blanched and sliced
- 250 grams peas, boiled
- 2 tblsps. khoya
- 1 cup grated coconut
- 1/2 cup cream
- 1 tomato grated
- 8 flakes of garlic, 1/2 inch piece ginger
- 4 green chillies
- 4 cardamoms, 4 cloves
- 50 grams paneer, cubed
- 1/4 tsp. turmeric powder
- Handful of chopped coriander leaves
- Salt and chilli powder to taste

Preparation

Fry khoya to a brown colour. Also fry mushrooms to a golden colour. Fry paneer. Grind coconut, ginger, garlic and chillies and coriander to a paste. Heat 4 tblsps. ghee and add cardamoms and cloves, then put in the ground tomato paste and cook till the ghee comes out of the mixture. Now put in khoya, cashewnuts, spices, mushrooms and mix the contents with 2 cups water. Cook till the gravy is reduced to half. Add peas, paneer and cream, and remove from fire after a few minutes. Decorate with almonds.

BANANA KOFTA CURRY

Ingredients (Serves 4)

For Koftas

- 6 raw bananas
- 1 tsp. grated ginger
- Handful of coriander leaves, ground
- 2 green chillies, ground
- 2 tblsps. cornflour
- 100 grams khoya
- 1 tblsps each of chopped cashewnuts and raisins
- 1/4 tsp. garam masala
- Salt to taste

For Curry

- 4 cloves, 4 cardamoms, 2 bay leaves
- 100 grams onions, grated
- 1 tsp. each of ginger and garlic paste
- 3 big tomatoes, grated
- 2 tblsps. ketchup
- 1/4 cup cream
- 1 tblsp dhania-jeera powder
- 1/4 tsp. turmeric powder
- Salt and chilli powder to taste

Preparation

Boil bananas and mix them with ginger, coriander leaves, green chillies and cornflour and salt. Knead these contents to a paste. Now mix together khoya, cashewnuts, raisins and garam masala. Make banana paste into balls around khoya mixture. Deep fry the balls to a golden colour. Heat 3 tblsps. ghee and add all the spices. Add ginger, garlic and onions and fry till soft. Add tomatoes, ketchup and spices. When the oil oozes out, put in 2 cups water. Boil for 10 minutes; mix in cream and pour over the koftas. Decorate with coriander leaves.

CORN KOFTA CURRY

Ingredients (Serves 4)

For Koftas

- 4 cups grated corn
- 1 cup milk
- Handful of chopped coriander leaves
- 2 green chillies, minced
- 1/4 tsp. grated ginger
- 2 tblsps. cornflour
- 100 grams grated cheese
- Salt and pepper to taste

For Curry

- 4 cloves, 4 cardamoms, 1 bay leaf
- 1/4 coconut, grated
- 25 grams groundnuts
- 1 tblsps. til
- 4 red kashmiri chillies
- 100 grams tomatoes, grated
- Handful of coriander leaves
- 1/4 tsp. turmeric powder
- 1 tblsp. dhania-jeera powder
- Salt to taste

Preparation

Fry corn in 1 tblsp. butter. Add the remaining kofta ingredients except cornflour and cheese. When the mixture turns completely dry, add cornflour and cheese. Form the mixture into small balls or koftas and deep fry the balls to a golden colour. Roast coconut, groundnuts, chillies and til and grind to a paste. Heat 4 tblsps. ghee, add the whole spices. Then add onion, ginger and garlic and fry till soft. Add coconut paste and all the spices and tomatoes and fry. When the oil comes out, put in 2 cups water. Bring to a boil, then reduce heat and cook for 5 minutes. Now pour the mixture over the koftas and decorate with coriander leaves.

CAULIFLOWER KOFTA CURRY

Ingredients (Serves 5)

For Koftas

- 1/2 kilo cauliflower, grated
- 4 tblsps. gramflour
- 1/2 tsp. cumin seeds, 1/2 tsp. grated ginger
- Handful of chopped coriander leaves
- 2 green chillies, minced
- Salt to taste

For Curry

- 250 grams grated tomatoes
- 250 grams green peas, boiled
- 1/2 tsp. cumin seeds
- 1 tsp. ginger strips
- 1 tblsp dhania-jeera powder
- 4 green chillies, slit
- 4 tblsps. cream
- 1/4 tsp. turmeric powder
- Salt and chilli powder to taste

Preparation

Mix all the kofta ingredients together. Form into small balls and deep fry the balls to a golden colour. Heat 4 tblsps. ghee, add cumin seeds, when they stop popping, add tomatoes, ginger, spices, salt and chillies. Cook the contents till the oil comes out. Now put in peas and 2 cups water. Boil for 10 minutes. Mix in cream and pour the mixture over the koftas. Decorate with coriander leaves.

Non-Vegetarian Curries

Fish Curry

Ingredients (Serves 4)

- 500 grams any white flesh fish like pomfret
- 250 grams tomatoes, pureed
- 1 medium onion, grated
- 6 flakes of garlic, grated
- 4 red and 4 green chillies
- 1 tsp. each of cumin and coriander seeds
- 1 tsp. garam masala
- 1/2 tsp. turmeric powder
- Salt to taste

Preparation

Clean the fish, cut it into slices and fry to a golden colour. Grind together chillies, cumin and coriander seeds, onion and garlic to make paste. Heat 2 tblsps. ghee and fry the ground paste; when it starts changing colour, add tomatoes, remaining spices and salt. Cook till the ghee oozes out, add fish and 2 cups of water. Cook the contents over a slow fire till the gravy becomes a little thick. Remove from fire and sprinkle on top garam masala and coriander leaves.

FISH KOFTA CURRY

Ingredients (Serves 5)

For Koftas

- 500 grams any white flesh fish boiled and flaked
- 1 onion, grated
- 1 tsp. each of grated ginger and garlic
- 3 slices of bread, soaked in water and squeezed dry
- Handful of coriander leaves
- 4 green chillies, minced
- 1 tsp. dhania-jeera power
- 1/2 tsp. garam masala
- Salt and chilli powder to taste

For Curry

- 100 grams onions, grated
- 1 tsp. each of ginger and garlic paste
- 250 grams pureed tomatoes
- 1/2 cup curd
- Handful of chopped coriander leaves
- 1/4 tsp. turmeric powder
- 1 tsp. dhania-jeera powder
- 1 tsp. garam masala
- Salt and chilli powder to taste

Preparation

Mix together all the kofta ingredients and form into round balls. Deep fry to a golden colour. Heat four tblsps. ghee and fry the paste to a golden colour. Add tomatoes and curd, spices and salt. When the ghee oozes out, add 2 cups of water. Bring the contents to a boil then reduce heat, add koftas and cook for 5 minutes. Decorate with coriander leaves and garam masala.

2

CURRIES OF UTTAR PRADESH

Among the Indian states, Uttar Pradesh has the highest population. Hindus and Muslims form two main communities of this state. Both these communities have influenced each other's food preparations and habits. The Muslim influence is quite marked on the non-vegetarian curries, which are generally prepared from mutton and chicken. But whether the curries are non-vegetarian or vegetarian, they are absolutely delicious. And, if eaten once cannot be easily forgotten.

Vegetarian Curries

Dahiwali Curry

Ingredients (Serves 6)

For Besan Wadies

- 250 grams besan or gramflour
- 50 grams ghee
- 100 grams curd
- 1 tblsp. poppy seeds
- 1/2 tblsp. crushed pomegranate seeds
- 1 tsp. grated ginger
- 2 green chillies, minced
- Handful of coriander leaves
- Salt and chilli powder to taste

For Curry

- 2 big cups curd beaten with 1 cup water
- 1/2 tsp. cumin seeds
- 1/4 tsp. turmeric powder
- Handful of coriander leaves
- 4 green chillies., slit
- 1 tblsp. dhania-jeera powder
- 1 inch piece ginger cut into strips
- Salt to taste

Preparation

Mix all the wadi ingredients together and form a dough. Roll out the dough into a 1/8th of an inch thick sheet. Cut the sheet into diamond shapes and deep fry to a golden colour. Heat 2 tblsps. oil and add cumin seeds and ginger. When the seeds stop tossing, add the wadies, chillies and all the spices. Mix well and then pour in the curd. Simmer for 10 minutes, sprinkle garam masala and coriander leaves on top. Serve hot.

Mango Curry

You can prepare this curry either from fresh mango juice or raw mango juice depending upon your choice.

Ingredients (Serves 8)

- 1 kilo mango juice of either raw or ripe mangoes
- 250 grams besan or gramflour
- 1 tsp. cumin seeds, 1/2 tsp. grated ginger
- A big pinch of asafoetida
- 1/2 tsp. black salt
- Handful of chopped coriander leaves
- 1 tblsp. dhania-jeera powder
- 1/2 tsp. shahjeera, or black jeera
- A pinch of soda bicarbonate
- Salt and chilli powder to taste
- 2 broken red chillies

Preparation

Mix besan with shahjeera, soda, black salt, ginger along with enough juice to form a thick batter. Heat enough ghee for deep frying to smoking. Lower the heat and drop the besan with the help of a teaspoon into the ghee. Deep fry the pakodas to a golden colour. Heat 2 tblsps. ghee and add asafoetida, cumin seeds and red chillies; when the seeds stop tossing, add pakodas and spices, pour in the mango juice. Cook for 5 minutes. Sprinkle on top, garam masala and coriander leaves.

BESAN KI CURRY

Ingredients (Serves 6)

For Wadies

- 250 grams besan
- 50 grams curd
- 50 grams ghee
- 1/2 tsp. crushed pomegranate seeds
- 1 tsp. ginger paste
- Handful of coriander leaves
- 1 tblsp. minced green chillies
- Salt and chilli powder to taste
- 1/2 tsp. each of crushed peppercorns, coriander and poppy seeds

For Curry

- 12 flakes of garlic, ground to a paste
- 1/2 tsp. mustard seeds
- 1 big tomato grated
- Handful of coriander leaves
- 1 tblsp. dhania-jeera powder
- 1/4 tsp. turmeric powder
- Salt and chilli powder to taste

Preparation

Mix all the wadi ingredients together. Add enough water to form a stiff dough. Roll the dough into long rolls. Boil the rolls in water for half an hour. Remove rolls from water and cut into round pieces. Heat 2 tblsps. ghee and add mustard seeds; When the seeds stop popping, add garlic, fry lightly and then add tomatoes, all the spices and salt. When the ghee oozes out, add wadies, mix well, add water in which the wadies were boiled. Cook till it becomes a little thick. Decorate with coriander leaves.

Karela Curry

Ingredients (Serves 5)

- 250 grams karela or bittergourds, peeled and sliced
- 100 grams tomatoes, grated
- 3 tblsps. besan or gramflour
- 1/2 tsp. cumin seeds
- 4 green chillies, slit
- Handful of coriander leaves
- 1 tblsp dhania-jeera powder
- 1 tsp. ginger strips
- 1/4 tsp. turmeric powder
- A big pinch of asafoetida
- Salt and chilli powder to taste

Preparation

Apply salt on karelas and set aside for a few hours. Then wash salted karelas in 3-4 changes of water. Deep fry karelas to a golden colour. Dissolve besan in 1 glass water. Heat 2 tblsps. oil and add asafoetida, ginger and cumin seeds. When the seeds stop tossing, add tomatoes and chillies, all the spices and salt. Cook till the oil comes out. Then add vegetables and besan. Cook till the curry becomes a little thick. Decorate with coriander leaves.

POTATO KOFTA CURRY

Ingredients (Serves 5)

For Koftas

- 250 grams potatoes, boiled, peeled and mashed
- 2 tblsps. cornflour
- For filling: 125 grams coarsely chopped boiled peas, 1 tblsp each of sliced cashewnuts and raisins
- 1/4 tsp. grated ginger
- 1/4 tsp. garam masala
- 2 green chillies, minced
- 2 tblsps. grated coconut
- Handful of finely sliced coriander leaves
- Salt to taste

For Curry

- 100 grams onions, grated
- 1/2 tsp. each grated ginger and garlic
- Handful of sliced coriander leaves
- 1/4 tsp. turmeric powder
- 1 tblsp dhania-jeera powder
- 1/2 tsp. each of cumin seeds and garam masala
- 2 tblsps. powder cashewnuts
- 2 tblsps. cream
- Salt and chilli powder to taste
- Decorate either with seedless grapes, ripe mango pieces or pineapple pieces

Preparation

Mix potatoes with cornflour and salt. Mix all the filling ingredients together. Form potato mixture into balls around the filling ingredients. Deep fry the balls to a golden colour. Now heat 3 tblsps. ghee and fry cumin seeds, then add ginger, garlic and onions and fry till the contents become soft. Then add tomatoes, spices, salt and cashewnuts. Cook till they become thick. Pour in 2 cups of water, boil for 5 minutes, mix in the cream and pour the curry over the koftas. Decorate with fruits of your choice.

NON-VEGETARIAN CURRIES

SHAHI KHEEMA KOFTA CURRY

Ingredients (Serves 4)

For Koftas

- 250 grams minced mutton or kheema
- 1/2 tsp. each of ginger and garlic paste
- 1/2 tsp. garam masala
- Handful of coriander leaves
- 1 egg, 2 green chillies, minced
- Salt and chilli powder to taste

For Curry

- 100 grams onions, grated
- 1 tsp. each of grated ginger and garlic
- 2 large tomatoes, grated
- 1 cup curd
- 1 tsp. garam masala
- 1 tblsp. dhania-jeera powder
- 1/4 tsp. turmeric powder
- 4 cloves, 4 cardamoms, 2 bay leaves
- 1-inch piece cinnamon stick
- Salt and chilli powder to taste

Preparation

Mix all the kofta ingredients together. Form the mixture into small balls and deep fry them to a golden colour. Heat 3 tblsps. ghee, add to it whole spices, then ginger, garlic and onions. Fry till the whole thing becomes soft. Add tomatoes, curd and spices. When the oil comes out, put in koftas, pour in 2 cups water and then cook over a slow fire for 5 minutes. Decorate with coriander leaves and sprinkle garam masala on top.

NAWABI KABAB CURRY

Ingredients (Serves 4)

For Kababs

- 250 grams minced mutton or kheema
- 100 grams chana dal
- 1 onion, 1/2 tsp. ginger and garlic paste
- Handful of coriander leaves
- 2 green chillies, minced
- 2 small eggs
- 1 tsp. garam masala
- Salt and chilli powder to taste

For Filling

- 1 cup curd, 2 tblsps. minced chillies
- 2 tblsps. minced onion, 1 tsp. minced ginger
- 2 tblsps. minced coriander leaves

For Curry

- 100 grams grated onions
- 1 tsp. grated ginger and garlic
- 250 grams grated tomatoes
- 1/2 tsp. cumin seeds
- 4 cloves, 4 cardamoms, 1 small piece cinnamon stick
- 1 tsp. garam masala
- 1 tblsp dhania-jeera powder
- Handful of coriander leaves
- Salt and chilli powder to taste

Preparation

Boil together all the kofta ingredients except eggs in salted water till tender and completely dry. Grind to a paste and mix in the eggs. Hang curd to remove all water. Beat the curd and mix it with rest of the filling ingredients. Form mutton mixture into balls around the filling. Deep fry the balls to a golden colour. Heat 4 tblsps. ghee and add in it all the spices. Also add ginger, garlic and onions and fry till the contents turn golden. Add tomatoes, spices and salt. When the mixture turns thick, pour in 2 cups of water. Boil for 10 minutes, pour it over the koftas, and sprinkle garam masala and coriander leaves on top. Serve hot.

Mirchiwale Ghosht ki Curry

Ingredients (Serves 5)

- 500 grams mutton, cut into serving portions
- 150 grams onions, grated
- 2 cups sour curd
- 1 tblsp. each of ginger and garlic paste
- 1 tblsp. dhania-jeera powder
- 1 tsp. garam masala
- 100 grams thick green chillies
- 1 tblsp each of mustard, cumin seeds and kalonji
- 1 tblsp each of black or shahjeera
- 1/4 tsp. fenugreek seeds
- Juice of lime
- Salt and chilli powder to taste

Preparation

Grind together all the whole spices. Mix them with lime juice, salt and chilli powder. Make a slit in each chilli halfway through and fill the chillies with the mixture. Fry to a light golden colour. Mix together the remaining ingredients along with 100 grams ghee. Cook the mixture over a slow fire till the mutton is done and dry. When the ghee comes on top, add 2 cups water and put in the chillies. Cook for another 5-7 minutes. Serve hot.

Kheema Mutton Curry

Ingredients (Serves 5)

- 500 grams minced mutton kheema
- 250 grams grated onions
- 250 grams green peas
- 1 tsp. each of ginger and garlic paste
- 1 tblsp. dhania-jeera powder
- 100 grams tomatoes, grated
- 150 grams beaten curd
- A few mint leaves
- 4 hard boiled eggs, shelled and halved
- 1 tblsp. garam masala, 1/4 tsp. turmeric powder
- 1 large handful chopped coriander leaves
- Salt and chilli powder to taste

Preparation

Heat 100 grams ghee and fry onion, ginger and garlic till soft. Add kheema and fry till dry and crumbly. Then add spices, salt, curd and tomatoes. Cook the mixture till it turns dry. Add peas and cover with hot water. When the kheema is cooked, remove from fire. Sprinkle on top coriander leaves, garam masala and decorate with sliced eggs.

3

MISCELLANEOUS CURRIES

To make this book a true representative of all the famous curries in India, I have given you in this section some famous curries of Rajasthan and Kashmir. Since these regions do not boast of many curries, I had to give your a few select ones for which they are famous. Rajputs are meat-eaters and they are fond of good things in life. Since they lived for long in close contact with Muslims, their curries have a distinct Muslim influence. Only after eating these curries, one marvels at their delicious taste. Besides Rajputs, another dominant community of Rajasthan is Marwaris. They are staunch vegetarians and they use pure ghee in most of their preparations. Marwari food is very simple. But in spite of all the simplicity, their gatta curry has gained national fame. The staple food of Kashmiris is rice which they eat with variety of meat curries. Amongst these curries, Yakhani curry is quite famous. It has a Persian influence on it. Yakhani curry is so delicious that once you eat it, you would like to eat it always. In this section, I couldn't resist including Coorgi mutton curry. It is a class of its own and very delicious.

SAFED MAS CURRY (RAJASTHAN)

Ingredients (Serves 4)

- 500 grams mutton, cut into serving portions
- 1/2 cup curd
- 1 tsp. ginger strips
- 2 tblsps. coconut paste
- 1 tsp. white pepper powder
- 1 tsp. white cardamom powder
- 12 cashewnuts, 12 almonds
- 4 tblsps. cream
- Few drops of rose essence
- 100 gms. ghee
- 1 tblsp. lime juice
- Salt to Taste

Preparation

Blanch almonds. Powder 8 almonds and 8 cashewnuts and slice the rest. Parboil mutton. Heat ghee, add mutton, curd, ginger, spice and salt. Cover the mixture with hot water and cook till mutton is tender and one-fourth of the gravy is left. Mix in lime juice, coconut and powdered nuts. Cook for 5 minutes. Remove the curry from fire, mix in rose essence and cream and decorate with nuts.

Gatta Curry (Rajasthan)

Ingredients (Serves 6)

For Gattas

- 2 cups gramflour
- 2 tblsps. ghee
- 1/2 tsp. cumin seeds and turmeric powder
- Salt and chilli powder to taste

For Curry

- 2 cups of sour curd
- 4 green chillies, slit
- 1 tsp. ginger strips
- 1/4 tsp. turmeric powder
- 2 tblsps. gramflour
- 1 tblsp. dhania-jeera powder
- 1/2 tsp. mustard seeds
- A few curry leaves
- Handful of coriander leaves
- Salt and chilli powder to taste
- 2 red chillies, broken

Preparation

Mix all the ingredients of gattas together with very little water to make a firm dough. Make long rolls of the dough and steam the rolls for half an hour. Cut the rolls into round pieces and fry them to a light golden colour. Beat the curd with 1 glass of water and gramflour. Heat 2 tblsps. ghee and add curry leaves, mustard seeds and red chillies. When the seeds stop tossing, add curd mixture, spices and chillies and cook till the curry turns a little thick. Put gattas in the curry and cook for a few more minutes. Decorate with coriander leaves.

MUGHLAI SHAMMI KABAB CURRY

Ingredients (Serves 5)

For Kababs

- 250 grams minced mutton or kheema
- 100 grams kidneys
- 1 egg, 50 grams chana dal
- 1 tsp. ginger and garlic paste
- 4 almonds, 4 cashewnuts, 1 tsp. each of charoli and raisins
- 1 tblsp. garam masala
- Handful of coriander leaves
- 1 onion, minced, a few mint leaves
- Salt and chilli powder to taste

For Gravy

- 100 grams grated onions
- 1 tblsp grated ginger
- 100 grams tomatoes, grated
- 1/8 tsp. saffron strands, soaked in 1 tblsp. hot milk
- 1/2 cup cream
- 25 grams each of pistachios, almonds and cashewnuts, powdered
- 1/2 cup coriander leaves, ground
- 1 tsp. garam masala
- 1 tsp. dhania-jeera powder
- Salt and chilli powder to taste

Preparation

To prepare kababs, soak dal for a few hours. Drain water and boil dal with meat and kidney. Cook till tender and dry. Grind the mixture to a smooth paste. Chop and fry nuts and raisins. Mix the beaten egg and all the kabab ingredients together except nuts. Make balls out of the mixture, place nuts at the centre of each ball. Deep fry balls to a golden colour. Heat 50 grams butter and fry onions and ginger till soft. Add tomatoes and coriander and ground paste of nuts. When the butter separates, put in 2 cups of water. Cook till the gravy turns a little thick. Now pour the curry over kababs. Top it with cream and saffron.

Kashmiri Yakhni Curry

Ingredients (Serves 6)

- 500 grams mutton ribs, cut into serving portions
- 100 grams grated onions
- 1 tsp. each of ginger and garlic paste
- 1/8 tsp. saffron strands, soaked in 1 tblsp. hot milk
- 1/4 litre milk
- 150 grams fresh curd
- 1 tblsp. garam masala
- 1 tblsp. dhania-jeera powder
- 1 tsp. roasted and powdered anise seeds and dry ginger powder
- 25 grams each of almonds and cashewnuts
- Silver warq (option)
- 1 tsp. cardamom powder
- Salt and chilli powder to taste

Preparation

Grind onions, ginger and garlic to a paste. Mix together curd and milk, and strain through a cloth. Boil mutton, strain out the stock and keep the mutton aside. Blanch and grind 3/4th of the nuts, slice the remaining nuts. Heat 50 grams ghee and fry onion, ginger and garlic to a red colour. Add mutton and fry it to a golden colour. Mix in the nuts, stock, milk mixture, spices and salt. When the gravy turns a little thick, remove the curry from fire. Sprinkle sliced nuts and saffron on top. Decorate with warq.

COORGI MUTTON CURRY

Ingredients (Serves 4)

- 500 grams mutton, cut into serving portions
- 150 grams small tomatoes
- 150 grams small potatoes, boiled and peeled
- 250 grams grated onions
- 1 tsp. each of ginger and garlic paste
- 4 green chillies, ground
- 1 tblsp. each of powdered cumin and coriander seeds
- Salt and chilli powder to taste

Preparation

Apply ginger, garlic and chillies to the mutton and set aside for half an hour. Heat 4 tblsps. oil and fry the onions till soft. Add mutton and all the spices and fry to a red colour. Cover the mixture with hot water and cook till the mutton is almost done. Then put in potatoes and tomatoes. When the mutton is cooked, remove the curry from fire. Decorate with coriander leaves and serve hot.

IMPORTANT INGREDIENTS USED IN CURRY PREPARATION AND THEIR MEDICINAL VALUE

Garlic

Garlic is a powerful antiseptic, and therefore it kills bacteria. It improves the voice and eyesight. It is a tonic to the hair and is useful in cough, gastric troubles, worms, heart disease, asthma, acidity, piles, chronic fever, loss of appetite, constipation, diabetes and tuberculosis. It also has properties of reducing high blood pressure.

Ginger

Ginger is good for eyes and throat. A small piece of ginger taken with a pinch of black salt before meals eliminates gas. It gives freedom from cough and cold and is also helpful in cardiac disorders, odema, urinary trouble, jaundice, piles and asthma. Ginger juice is also said to prevent the malignancy of the tongue and the throat. Toothache is also relieved if a piece of ginger is rubbed on the painful tooth.

Onions

From the medicinal point of view, white onions are more beneficial to the body than other varieties. They increase virility and induce sleep. They are good for curing tuberculosis, piles, leprosy, swelling and blood impurities. One is saved from sunstroke if one regularly eats raw onions during hot season. Eating raw onion in the morning and at bedtime is good for jaundice patients.

Coriander leaves

Coriander leaves are mostly used for decorating a dish or preparing chutney. They give a special flavour to food. Coriander is not only fragrant and appetizing but also a good digestive aid. It has a cooling effect on our body, and is good for vision and agreeable to the heart.

Mint

Mint is usually made into chutneys or sometimes put in non-vegetarian dishes. It is not only palatable and appetizing but is also good for heart. It expels gas and is useful in cough, dysentery, gastroenteritis and diarrhoea.

Vegetables

They are extremely rich source of minerals, enzymes and vitamins. Their nutritional value varies according to their different parts. Leaves, stems and fruits are rich sources of minerals, vitamins, water and roughage, whereas seeds are high in carbohydrates and proteins. Greener and fresher the vegetables, higher their vitamin content. Therefore always go in for fresh vegetables available in the market.

Eggs

Eggs are a valuable source of animal proteins and next to milk in providing nutrition. Egg yolk contains Iron, B vitamins, calcium and a considerable amount of proteins. White portion contains vitamin B and more than half the amount of proteins in egg. Patients of high cholesterol and heart disease should not eat yolks but go only for whites of the egg.

Fish

Fish rates high in nutritional value. It supplies proteins which are more easily digestible than the proteins of meat. Fish gives fat, vitamins A & D and minerals like iodine and copper to the body. Fish is a low-fat form of proteins. Sardines, mackerel and other oily fish contain omega-3 fatty acids that help clear the body of cholesterol.

Meat & Poultry

These are very rich sources of proteins. Besides proteins they are rich in fats, vitamin A and phosphorus. However, kidney and liver are low in fat. Just one helping a day of meat or fish is enough for the daily body requirement of proteins.

FOODGRAINS

Cookery Glossary

English	Spiked millet	Barley	Jowar	Italian millet	Maize (dry)	Oatmeal	Ragi
Hindi	Bajra	Jau	Juar-janera	Kangri	Makai	Jai	Okra
Tamil	Cambu	Barli arisi	Cholam	Thenai	Muka cholam	—	Ragi
Telugu	Gantelu	Barli biyyam	Jonnalu	Korralu	Mekka jonnalu	—	Chollu
Marathi	Bajri	Juv	Jwari	Rala	Muka	Jai	Nachni
Bengali	Bajra	Job	Juar	Syamadhan kangni	Sukna paka bhutta	—	—
Gujarati	Bajri	Jau	Juar	Ral kang	Makai	—	Ragi bhav
Malayalam	Kamboo	Yavam	Cholam	Thina	Unakku cholam	Oat mavu	Moothari (korra)
Kannada	—	—	Jola	—	Vonugida musikinu	Jolu	Ragi
Kashmiri	Baajr'u	Wushku	—	Shol	Makka'y	—	—

Contd...

English	Rice (raw)	Rice (parboiled)	Rice (white)	Rice (black)	Rice flakes	Rice (puffed)	Samai
Hindi	Arwa chawal	Usna chawal	Safed chaval	Chaval (kala)	Chowla	Murmura	Kutki, Sanwali
Tamil	Pachai arisi	Puzhungal arisi	Vellai puttu arisi	Karuppu puttu arisi	Arisi aval	Arisia pori	Samai
Telugu	Pachi biyyam	Uppudu biyyam	Thella biyyam	Nalla biyyam	Atukulu	Murmuralu	—
Marathi	Tandool	Tandool ukda	—	—	Pohe	Murmure	Sava
Bengali	Atap chowl	Siddha chowl	—	—	Chaler khood	Muri	Kangni
Gujarati	Hatna	Ukadelloo chokha	—	—	Pohva	Mumra	—
Malayalam	Pacchari	Puzhungal ari	Velutha puttari	Krutha puttari	Avil	Pori	—
Kannada	Kotnuda	Kotnuda	—	—	Avalukki	—	Puri
Kashmiri	—	—	—	—	—	—	—

Contd...

English	Semolina	Vermicelli	Wheat (whole)	Wheat flour (whole)	Wheat flour (refined)	Wheat (broken)
Hindi	Sooji	Siwain	Gehun	Atta	Maida	Daliya
Tamil	Ravai	Semiya	Godumai	Muzhu godnai ma	Maida mavu	Godhumbi ravai
Telugu	Rawa	Semiya	Godhumalu	Godhum pindi	Maidha pindi	Dinchina gadhumalu
Marathi	–	Shevaya	Gahu	Gahu kuneek	Gahu kuneek	Gavache satva
Bengali	Suji	Sewai	Gomasta	Atta	Maida	Bhanga gom
Gujarati	–	–	Ghau	Ato	–	Fadia ghaun
Malayalam	Rava	Semiya	Muzhu gothambou	Gothambu mavu	Maidu tha gothambu mavu	Gothumbu ari
Kannada	–	Shavige	Godhi	Godhi	Hittu madia	Kuttida Godhi
Kashmiri	–	Ku' nu'	–	–	–	–

VEGETABLES

English	Ash gourd	Bitter gourd	Bottle gourd	Brinjal	Broad beans	Cabbage	Capsicum
Hindi	Safed petha	Karela	Chia	Baingan	Sem	Bandhgobi	Simla mirch
Bengali	Chal kumdo	karala	Laoo	Begoon	Sheem	Badha kopee	Lonka
Assamese	Lao bishesh	–	Jati lao	Bengena	Urahi	Bondhakobi	Kashmiri jalakai
Oriya	Pani kakkaru	–	Lau	Baigana	Shimba	Patrokobi	Simla lonka
Marathi	Kohala	Karle	Dudhi	Wangi	Ghewda	Pan kobi	Bhopli mirchi
Gujarati	Petha	Karela	Dudhi	Ringna	Papdi	Kobi	Simla marchan
Telugu	Boodie gumadi	Kakara	Sorakaya	Vankaya	Pedda chikkudu	Kosu	Pedda mirappa
Kannada	Budu gumbala	Hagalkai	Sorekai	Badanekai	Chapparadavare	Kosu	Donne minasinakai
Tamil	Pooshanikkai	Pavakkai	Suraikai	Kaththarikai	Avaraikai	Muttaikosu	Kuda milakai
Malayalam	Kumbalanga	Kaypakka	Cheraikai	Vazhutheninga	Amarakai	Muttakose	Parangi mulagu
Kashmiri	Masha'ly al	Karelu	–	Waangun	–	Bandgobhi	–

Contd...

English	Carrot	Cauliflower	Cluster beans	Colocasia	Coriander leaves	Cucumber	Curry leaves
Hindi	Gajar	Phulgobi	Guar ki phalli	Arvi	Hara Dhania	Khira	Kadi patta
Bengali	Gujar	Foolcopy	Jhar sim	–	Dhonay pata	Sasha	Curry pata
Assamese	Gajor	Phoolkobi	–	Kochu	Dhania paat	–	Narasingha paat
Oriya	Gajar	Phulakobi	–	–	Dhania patra	–	Bhrusanga patta
Marathi	Gajar	Fulkobi	Govari	Alu kanda	Kothimbir	Kakari	Kadhi patta
Gujarati	Gajar	Fool kobi	Govar	Alvi	Kothmir	Kakdi	Mitho limdo
Telugu	Gajjara	Cauliflower	Goruchikkudu kayalu	Chamadumpa	Kothimeera	Dosakaya	Karivepaku
Kannada	Gajjari	Hookosu	Gorikayi	Keshave	Kottambari soppu	Southaikayi	Karibevu
Tamil	Carrot	Koveppu	Kothavarangai	Seppann kizhangu	Koththamali ilaigal	Kakkarikkai	Kariveppilai
Malayalam	Carrot	Coliflower	Kothavara	Chembu	Kothamalli ila	Vellari	Kariveppila
Kashmiri	–	Phoolgobhi	–	–	–	Laa'r	–

Contd...

English	Drumstick	French beans	Garlic	Ginger (fresh)	Green chillies	Jackfruit	Lady's finger
Hindi	Sahjan ki phali	Pharsbeen	Lassan	Adrak	Hari mirch	Kathal	Bhindi
Bengali	Sajane dauta	French beans	Rasoon	Ada (tatka)	Kancha lonka	Echore	Dhanroce
Assamese	Sajina	Faras been	Naharoo	Ada (kesa)	Kesa jalakia	–	Bhendi
Oriya	Sajana chhuin	French beans	Rasuna	Ada (kancha)	Kancha lonka	–	Bhendi
Marathi	Shevgyachya shenga	Farasbi	Lasun	Aale	Hirvya mirchya	Kawla phanas	Bhendi
Gujarati	Saragvani shing	Fansi	Lasan	Adu	Lila marcha	Phunas	Bhinda
Telugu	Munagakayalu	French chikkudu	Vellulli	Allam (pachchi)	Pachchi mirapakayalu	Letha panasa	Bendakaaya
Kannada	Nuggekai	Avare	Bellulli	Ashi Shunti	Hasi menasinakai	Yele halasu	Bendekai
Tamil	Murungaikai	Beans	Ulli Poondu	Inji	Pachchai milagai	Pila pinchu	Vendaikai
Malayalam	Muringakkaya	Beans	Veluthulli	Inji	Pachamulagu	Idichakka	Vendakka
Kashmiri	–	–	Ruhan	–	Myool martsu waungun	–	Bindu

Contd...

English	Lettuce	Lemon	Mint leaves	Onion	Parwal	Peas	Plantain flower	Plantain green
Hindi	Salad ke patte	Nimbu	Pudina	Pyaz	Parwal	Matar	Kele ka phool	Kacha kela
Bengali	Lettuce	Lebu	Poodina pata	Pyaz	Potol	Motor	Mocha	Kancha kala
Assamese	Laipaat	Nemu	Podina	–	Patol	Motormah	–	–
Oriya	Lettuce	Lembu	Podana patra	–	Potala	Matar	–	–
Marathi	Saladchi paane	Limbu	Pudina	Kanda	–	Matar	Kel phool	Kele
Gujarati	Lettuce	Limbu	Fudino	Dungli	–	Vatana	Kelphool	Kela
Telugu	Lettuce koora	Nimma	Pudhina koora	Nirulli	–	Bathanedu	Aratipuwu	Arati kayi
Kannada	Lettuce soppu	Nimbu	Pudina sopu	Erulli	–	Betani	Balo mothu	Bala kayi
Tamil	Lettuce keerai	Elumicham pazham	Pudhinaa	Vengayam	–	Pattani	Vazhaippu	Vazhaikkai
Malayalam	Uvarcheera	Cherunaranga	Pudhinaa	Ulli	–	Pattani Payaru	Vazhappoo	Vazhakka
Kashmiri	Salaad	–	–	Gandu	–	Matar	–	–

Contd...

English	Plantain stem	Potato	Radish	Red pumpkin	Ridge gourd	Snake gourd	Sweet potato	Yam elephant
Hindi	Kele ka tana	Aloo	Muli	Sitaphal	Torai	–	Shakarkand	Zaminkand
Bengali	Thor	Aloo	Mulo	Ronga Koomra	Jhinge	Chichinga	Rangalu	Kham aloo
Assamese	–	Alu	–	Ronga lao	–	–	–	Kaath aloo
Oriya	–	Alu	–	Kakharu	–	–	–	Deshi alu
Marathi	Kelecha khunt	Batate	Mula	Lal bhopla	Dodka	Pudwal	Ratale	Suran
Gujarati	Kelanu thed	Batata	Mula	Kolu	Turai	Pandola	Sakkaria	Suran
Telugu	Arati davva	Bangaala dumpa	Mullangi	Erra gummadi	Beerakai	Potlakayi	Dumpalu	Kanda dumpa
Kannada	Dindu	Aalugadde	Mullangi	Kempu kumbala	Heeraikai	Padavalai	Genasu	Suvamagadde
Tamil	Vazhaithandu	Urulaikizhangu	Mullangi	Parangikai	Pirrkkankai	Podalangai	Sarkarai valli kizhangu	Chenai kizhangu
Malayalam	Vazhappindi	Uralakkizhangu	Mullangi	Chuvappu mathan	Pecchinga	Padavalanga	Chakkara kizhangu	Chena
Kashmiri	–	Oloo	Muj	Paarimal	Turrelu	–	–	–

PULSES

English	Bengal gram (whole)	Bengal gram (split)	Black gram (split)	Black gram (whole)	Cornflour	Cow gram	Green gram (whole)
Hindi	Chana	Chana dal	Urad dal	Sabat urad	Makai ka atta	Lobia (bada)	Moong
Bengali	Chola	Banglar chhola	Mashkolair dal	Mashkolai dal	Bhoottar maida	Barbati	Mug
Assamese	—	Buttor dail	Matir dail (phola)	Matir dail (gota)	Moida	—	—
Oriya	Buta (chhota)	Buta (chhota)	Biri (phala)	Biri (gota)	Makka atta	—	—
Marathi	Hurbhura	Chana dal	Udid dal	Udid	Makyache pith	Kuleeth	Mug
Gujarati	Chana	Chana nidaal	Adad ni dal	Adad	Makai no lot	—	Mag
Telugu	Sanagalu	Senaga pappu	Mina pappu	Minu mulu	Mokkajonnalu (pindi)	Ada chandalu	Pesalu
Kannada	Kadale	Kadale bela	Uddina bela	Uddu	Musukinajolada hittu	Thadaguni	Hesaru kalu
Tamil	Muzhu kadalai	Kadalai paruppu	Ulutham paruppu	Ulundhu	Chola Maavu	Karamani	Pachai payaru
Malayalam	Kadala	Kadala parippu	Uzhunnu parippu	Uzhunnu	Cholapodi	Payar	Cherupayaru
Kashmiri	Chanu	—	Maha	—	—	—	Muang

Contd...

English	Green gram (split)	Horse gram	Kesari dal	Kidney beans	Red gram	Red lentils	Soya bean
Hindi	Moong dal	Kulthi	Lang dal	Rajma	Arhar dal	Masoor dal	Bhat
Bengali	—	Kulthi kalai	Khesari	Barbati beej	Arhar dal	Lal masoor (bhanga)	Gari kalai
Assamese	—	—	—	Markhowa urahi	Rahor dail	Masoor dail (phola)	—
Oriya	—	—	—	Baragudi chhuin	Harada dali	Masura dali (phala)	—
Marathi	—	Kuleeth	Lakh dal	—	Tur dal	Masur dal	Soya
Gujarati	—	Kuleeth	Lakh	—	Tuver dal	Masur dal	Soya
Telugu	Pesaru pappu	Ulavalu	Lamka pappu	—	Kandi pappu	Missu pappu	—
Kannada	Hesare bele	Huruli	—	—	Togar bele	Masur bele	—
Tamil	Pasi paruppu	Kollu	Vattuparuppu	—	Thuvaram parappu	Massor paruppu	—
Malayalam	Cherupayar parippu	Muthira	—	—	Thuvara parippu	Masoor parippu	Soya bean
Kashmiri	—	—	—	—	—	Musur	—

Fruits and Dry Fruits

English	Almond	Coconut	Currants	Dates	Dry plums
Hindi	Badam	Nariyal	Mungaqqa	Khajur	Alu bukhara
Bengali	Badam	Narcole	Manaca	Khejoor	Sookno kool
Assamese	Badam	Narikol	Kismis	Khejur	Sukan bogori
Oriya	Badaam	Nadia	Kala kismis	Khajura	Barakoli jateeya phala
Marathi	Badam	Naral	Manuka	Khajur	Alubhukar
Gujarati	Badam	Naliyer	Kalli draksh	Khajoor	Suka Plum
Telugu	Badam	Kobbari kaaya	Endu nalla dhraksha	Kharjoora pandu	–
Kannada	Badami	Tenginakai	Dweepa dharakshi-kappu	Kharjoora	–
Tamil	Badam/vadhumai	Thengai	Karumdhraakshai	Perichampazham	Aalpacota ular pazham
Malayalam	Badam	Nalikeram/Thenga	Karuthamurthiri	Eethapazham	–

Contd...

English	Guavas	Lemon	Orange	Raisins	Walnuts
Hindi	Amrud	Nimbu	Santra	Kishmish	Akhrot
Bengali	Payara	Lebu	Kamla lebu	Kishmish	Akhrot
Assamese	Madhurium	Nemu	Sumothira	Sukan angoor	Akhrot
Oriya	Piiuli	Lembu	Kamala	Kismis	Akhrot
Marathi	Peru	Limbu	Santre	Bedane	Akrod
Gujarati	Jamrukh	Limbu	Santara	Lal draksh	Akhrot
Telugu	Jaamapandu	Nimma	Kamala Pandu	Kismis pallu	Aakrot
Kannada	Seebe	Nimbe	Kittale	Dweepadrakshi	Acrota
Tamil	Koyyapazham	Elumicham pazham	Kichilipazham	Ular dhraakshai	Akhrot
Malayalam	Perakkai	Cherunaranga	Madhura naranga	Unakkamunthiri	Akrotandi

Contd...

Dry Spices

English	Aniseed	Asafoetida	Basil leaves	Bay leaf	Caraway seeds	Cardamom (brown)	Cardamom (green)	Cinnamon
Hindi	Saunf	Hing	Tulse ke patte	Tej patta	Shahjeera	Moti elaichi	Choti elaichi	Dalchini
Bengali	Mowri	Hing	Tulsi pata	Tej pata	Sajeera	Elach (tamate)	Elach (sobooj)	Daroochini
Assamese	Guwamori	Hing	Tulosi paat	Teipaat	Bilati jira	Ilachi (muga)	Ilachi (sevjia)	Dalcheni
Oriya	Panamahuri	Hengu	Tulasi patra	Teja patra	Sahajira	Aleicha	Gijuratie	Dalachini
Marathi	Badishep	Hing	Tulsichi paney	Tamal patra	Shahjeera	Masala welchi	Welchi (hirvi)	Dalchini
Gujarati	Variyali	Hing	Tulsina pan	Tamal patra	Jiru	Elcho	Lila alchi	Tuj
Telugu	Sopaginja	Inguva	Thulasi akulu	–	Seema sopyginjae	Yalakulu	Yala kulu (pachavi)	Dalchina chekka
Kannada	Sopubeeja	Hingu	Tulasi ele	–	Caraway beejagalre	Yalakki	Yalakki (hasuru)	Dalchini
Tamil	Perumjeerakam	Perungaayam	Thulasi	–	Karunjeerakam	Elakkai (Pazhuppu)	Elakkai (pachchai)	Lavangapattai
Malayalam	Perumjeerakam	Kaayam	Tulasi	–	Karunjeerakam	Elakkaya	Pach Elakkaya	Karuvapatta
Kashmiri	–	Yangu	–	–	–	Aal budu'a aal	–	–

Contd...

English	Cloves	Coriander seeds	Cumin seeds	Fenugreek seeds	Mace	Mustard seeds	Nutmeg	Parsley
Hindi	Laung	Sukha dhania	Jeera	Methi dana	Javitri	Rai	Jaiphal	Ajmooda ka patta
Bengali	Labango	Dhonay	Jeera	Methi	Jaeetri	Sarsay	Jaifall	Parsley
Assamese	Long	Dhania guti	Gota jeera	Paleng	Janee	Sarioh guti	Jaaiphal	Sugandhi lota
Oriya	Labanga	Dhania	Jira	Methi	Jayatree	Sorisha	Jaiphala	Balabalua shaga
Marathi	Lavanga	Dhane	Jire	Methi dane	Jaypatri	Mohari	Jayphal	Ajmoda
Gujarati	Laving	Dhana	Jeeru	Methi	Jaypatra	Rai	Jaypal	Ajmo
Telugu	Lavangalu	Dhaniyalu	Jeelakara	Menthulu	Japathri	Aavaalu	Jaikaaya	Kothimeerajati koora
Kannada	Lavanga	Kottambari beeja	Jeerige	Menthe	Japatri	Sasive kalu	Jaika	Kottambari jotiya soppu
Tamil	Kraambu	Koththamali virai	Jeerakam	Vendhayam	Jaadipathri	Kadugu	Jaadhikai	Kothamalu ilaigal pole
Malayalam	Karayaamboovu	Kothamalli	Jeerakam	Uluva	Jathipathri	Kadugu	Jathikka	Malliela pole
Kashmiri	Ru'ang	Daaniwal	Zyur	–	Jalwatur	–	Zaaphal	–

45

English	Peppercorns	Pomegranate seeds	Poppy seeds	Red Chillies	Tamarind	Turmeric	Vinegar	Thymol
Hindi	Kali mirch ke daane	Anardana	Khus khus	Lal mirch	Imli	Haldi	Sirka	Ajwain
Bengali	Marich	Dareem bij	Posto	Paka lonka	Tentool	Halood	Seerka	–
Assamese	Jaluk	Dalim guti	–	Sukan jalakia	Teteli	Halodhi	Sirka	–
Oriya	Golamaricha	Dalimba manji	–	Nali lankamaricha	Tentuli	Haladi	Vinegar	–
Marathi	Kale Miri	Dalimbache dane	Khas khas	Lal mirchya	Chincha	Halad	Sirka	Onva
Gujarati	Mari	Dadamna bee	Khaskhas	Lal marcha	Amli	Haldar	Sirko	–
Telugu	Miriyaalu	Daanimma ginjalu	Casagasaalu	Erra mirapa kayalu	Chinthapandu	Pasupu	–	–
Kannada	Menasina kalu	Dalimbo beeja	Casagase beeja	Kempu menasinakai	Hunase hannu	Arasina	–	–
Tamil	Milagu	Maadhulai vidhai	Kasakasaa	Milagai vatal	Puli	Manjal	Pulikaadi	–
Malayalam	Kurumulagu	Madhala naranga kuru	Kaskas	Chavanna Mulagu	Puli	Manjal	Vinagiri	–

SELF-IMPROVEMENT/PERSONALITY DEVELOPMENT

Also Available
in Hindi

Also Available
in Hindi

Also Available
in Kannada, Tamil

Also Available
in Kannada

Also Available
in Kannada